1001 Jazz Licks

A Complete Jazz Vocabulary for the Improvising Musician
by Jack Shneidman

ISBN 978-1-57560-278-3

Visit our website at www.cherrylane.com

INTRODUCTION

The jazz lick is one of the most important tools of improvisation. In addition to a thorough knowledge of chords and scales, all the great jazz players have a large vocabulary of these short melodic phrases, which they incorporate in their improvised solos. The jazz player uses licks the same way we use simple or common phrases in speech. In short, licks are basic musical statements an improviser calls upon to meet the musical demands of the moment.

With this huge book in your hand, you might be asking yourself, "Where do I start?" Well, it's helpful to notice that this book is divided into three main sections: *Essential Licks*, *Stylistic Licks*, and *Licks over Standard-Type Progressions*.

Essential Licks (licks 1-560) is comprised of licks that are played over either a single chord, a standard harmonic progression, or a particular mode. All the licks are written in the key of C. In the case of licks that are based on modes, the key signature of the parent scale is given. For example, all C Dorian licks have the key signature of B♭ major, because C Dorian is the mode built on the second scale degree of the B♭ major scale. C Lydian, to name another example, is built on the fourth degree of the G major scale therefore it will bear the key signature of G major.

Stylistic Licks (licks 561-800) is based on the idiomatic traits of different eras in jazz history. For example, the licks from the swing era resemble the work of master tenor saxophonists Lester Young, Coleman Hawkins, as well as the great guitarist Charlie Christian. The licks from the bebop era are based on the styles of saxophonists Charlie Parker, Sonny Stitt, and Sonny Rollins, the pianist Bud Powell, and trumpeters Dizzy Gillespie and Clifford Brown. Some of the players representative of the hard bop era include pianists Horace Silver and Bobby Timmons, tenor saxophonists Hank Mobley and Dexter Gordon, and trumpeters Kenny Dorham and Blue Mitchell. The licks in the post bop section pay homage to the harmonically advanced sounds of tenor saxophonists John Coltrane and Joe Henderson, pianists McCoy Tyner and Herbie Hancock, and trumpeters Freddie Hubbard and Woody Shaw. All of the harmonic progressions that are utilized in this section are standard progressions. The remainder of this section (non-harmonic, and fusion/funk licks) demonstrates some of the intervalic and harmonic concepts of today's greatest contemporary jazz musicians. These include saxophonists Dave Liebman, Michael Brecker, and Kenny Garrett, guitarist John Scofield, and pianist Chick Corea.

Licks over Standard-Type Progressions (licks 801-1001) is comprised of licks played over the opening four bars of twenty standard-type tunes. These phrases feature a wide variety of harmonic progressions, some different time signatures ($_3$ and $_6$), and some material that has a Brazilian or Afro-Cuban flavor ("New Bossa," and "Night under Anesthesia," respectively).

All the licks in this book have chord symbols above them given in their most basic form (only the root and the chord quality are named). Some of these licks are very advanced and include a liberal usage of chromaticism, substitute scales and modes, implied passing chords, and entire cycles of substitute harmonies. Don't let this intimidate you; the logic and expressive options they offer will become clearer with time and a little patient study.

How to Use this Book

This book is not meant to be read through from cover to cover. It is recommended that you devote a concentrated amount of time and study to mastering major and minor ii-V-I's: These progressions are the basic building blocks for numerous jazz standards. Do not feel the need to master each individual lick, find the ones that you like and focus your attention on them, concentrate on what is immediately valuable to you. Once you have comfortably learned one of the licks, transpose it to all of the remaining eleven keys. Try to find different ways for the lick to begin or end and experiment with different phrasings and articulations.

1001 Jazz Licks is written with the idea of giving you some insight into the melodic vocabulary of jazz and broaden your awareness of the harmonic possibilities available. All of this is in hope of helping you to cultivate your own, unique sense of melody and harmony. Have fun!

Acknowledgments

I would like to thank my editors, Arthur Rotfeld and Toby Wine, for their vision, profound knowledge, and patience. Additional thanks go out to Nick Trautwein and Cherry Lane author Joe Chaurpakorn. Finally, a very special thanks go to my friends and family for their unyielding support.

About the Author

Jack Scneidman is a guitarist, composer, and arranger who lives and works in the New York Metropolitan area. He has studied with Ron Carter, Mike Longo, and Rob Schwimmer, guitarists Gene Bertoncini and Ken Wessell, and Pulitzer Prize winning composer David del Tredici. Jack plays with a variety of jazz combos on the New York club scene and around the world.

ESSENTIAL LICKS

STYLISTIC LICKS

E N T S

LICKS OVER STANDARD-TYPE PROGRESSIONS

11 Cmaj7

12 Cmaj7

13 Cmaj7

14 Cmaj7

15 Cmaj7

16 Cmaj7

17 Cmaj7

18 Cmaj7

19 Cmaj7

20 Cmaj7

31

32

33

34

35

36

37

38

39

40

41

42

43

44

45

46

47

48

49

50

51

52

53

54

55

56

57

58

59

60

61

62

63

64

65

66

67

68

69

70

71

72

73

74

75

76

77

78

79

80

91

92

93

94

95

96

97

98

99

100

111

112

113

114

115

116

117

118

119

120

121

122

123

124

125

126

127

128

129

130

131

132

133

134

135

136

137

138

139

140

141

142

143

144

145

146

147

148

149

150

151

152

153

154

155

156

157

158

159

160

161

162

163

164

165

166

167

168

169

170

171

172

173

174

175

176

177

178

179

180

191

192

193

194

195

196

197

198

199

200

201

202

203

204

205

206

207

208

209

210

211

212

213

214

215

216

217

218

219

220

221

222

223

224

225

226

227

228

229

230

231

232

233

234

235

236

237

238

239

240

241

242

243

244

245

246

247

248

249

250

251

252

253

254

255

256

257

258

259

260

261

262

263

264

265

266

267

268

269

270

271

272

273

274

275

276

277

278

279

280

281

282

283

284

285

286

287

288

289

290

291

292

293

294

295

296

297

298

299

300

01

02

03

304

305

306

307

308

309

310

311

312

313

314

315

316

317

318

319

320

321

322

323

324

325

326

327

328

329

330

331

332

333

334

335

336

337

338

339

340

341

342

343

344

345

346

347

348

349

350

351

352

353

354

355

356

357

358

359

360

361

362

363

364

365

366

367

368

369

370

371

372

373

374

375

376

377

378

379

380

381

382

383

384

385

386

387

388

389

390

391

392

393

394

395

396

397

398

399

400

401

402

403

404

405

406

407

408

409

410

411

412

413

414

415

416

417

418

419

420

421

422

423

424

425

426

427

428

429

430

431

432

433

434

435

436

437

438

439

440

441

442

443

444

445

446

447

448

449

450

451

452

453

454

455

456

457

458
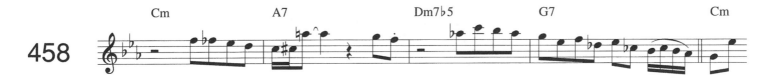

459

460

461

462

463

464

465

466

467

468

469

470

471

472

473

474

475

476

477

478

479

480

481
Cmaj7#11

482
Cmaj7#11

483
Cmaj7#11

484
Cmaj7#11

485
Cmaj7#11

486
Cmaj7#11

487
Cmaj7#11

488
Cmaj7#11

489
Cmaj7#11

490
Cmaj7#11

491
Cmaj7#11

492
Cmaj7#11

493
Cmaj7#11

494
Cmaj7#11

495
Cmaj7#11

496
Cmaj7#11

497
Cmaj7#11

498
Cmaj7#11

499
Cmaj7#11

500
Cmaj7#11

511

512

513

514

515

516

517

518

519

520

521

Cm7

522

Cm7

523

Cm7

524

Cm7

525

Cm7

526

Cm7

527

Cm7

3

528

Cm7

529

Cm7

530

Cm7

531

532

533

534

535

536

537

538

539

540

551

552

553

554

555

556

557

558

559

560

STYLISTIC LICKS

561
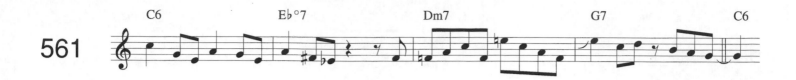

562

563

564

565

566

567

568

569

570

571

572

573

574

575

576

577

578

579

580

581

582

583

584

585

586

587

588

589

590

591

592

593

594

595

596

597

598

599

600

601

602

603

604

605

606

607

608

609

610

611

612

613

614

615

616

617

618

619

620

621

622

623

624

625

626

627

628

629

630

631

632

633

634

635

636

637

638

639

640

641

642

643

644

645

646

647

648

649

650

651

652

653

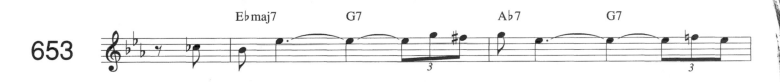

654

655

656

657

658

659

660

661

662

663

664

665

666

667

668

669

670

671

672

673

674

675

676

677

678

679

680

681

682

683

684

685

686

687

688

689

690

691

692

693

694

695

STYLISTIC LICKS

696

Dm7

697

Dm7

698

Dm7

699

Dm7

700

Dm7

701

B♭maj7♯11 Am7

702

B♭maj7♯11 Am7

703

B♭maj7♯11 Am7

704

B♭maj7♯11 Am7

705

B♭maj7♯11 Am7

706

B♭maj7♯11 Am7

718

719

720

721

722

723

724

725

726

727

728

STYLISTIC LICKS

761

762

763

764

765

766

767

774

775

776

777

778

779

785

786

787

788

789

790

796

797

798

799

800

801

802

803

804

805

806

807

808

809

810

811

812

813

814

815

816

817

818

819

820

821

822

823

824

825

826

827

828

829

830

831

832

833

834

835

836

837

838

839

840

841

842

843

844

845

846

847

848

849

850

851

852

853

854

855

856

857

858

859

860

861

862

863

864

865

866

867

868

869

870

871

872

873

874

875

876

877

878

879

880

881

882

883

884

885

886

887

888

889

890

891

892

893

894

895

896

897

898

899

900

901

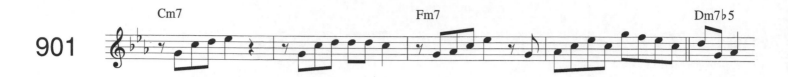

902

903

904

905

906

907

908

909

910

911

912

913

914

915

916

917

918

919

920

921

922

923

924

925

926

927

928

929

930

931

932

933

934

935

936

937

938

939

940

941

942

943

944

945

946

947

948

949

950

951

952

953

954

955

956

957

958

959

960

961

962

963

964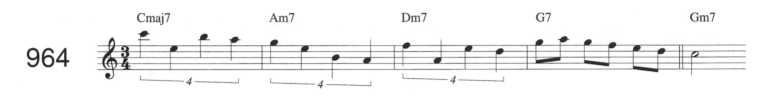

965

966

967

968

969

970

971

972

973

974

975

976

977

978

979

980

981

982

983

984

985

986

987

988

989

990

991

992

993

994

995

996

997

998

999

1000

1001

INDEX

Essential Licks

Stylistic Licks

Licks over Standard-Type Progressions